PRECIOUS Gems

A Collection of Poetic Expressions

Professor Sue C

ISBN
978-1-956529-66-1 (Paperback)
978-1-956529-65-4 (eBook)

Contents

Why I Write.. 1

Has Anyone Ever Loved You?... 2

Reflection 4

Ciera 5

So. Cal Blues 6

I watch as they 8

Soaring.. 10

I Wait..11

Chicken Pox.. 13

The Desert at Night...15

Her 17

Her- Twenty Years Previous... 18

Free to Be..19

Fear the Beasts No Longer 20

Why I Write

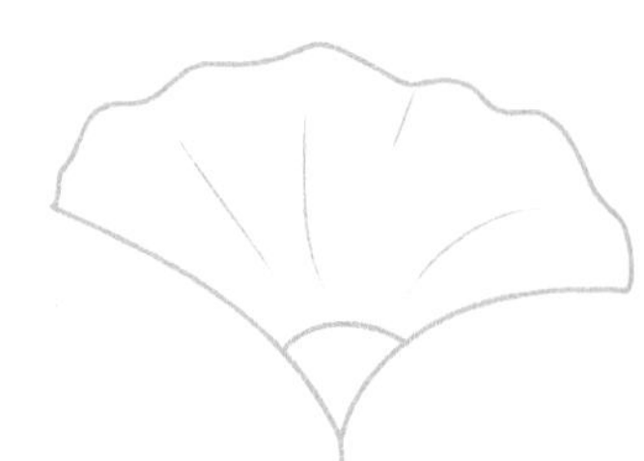

It's been so long since I have written,

Now half the night I've spent here sitting,

Part of me is back alive,

Now I know I can survive,

Never realizing how much was paper and lead,

It's through these words my soul is fed,

It is my laughter, it is my song,

It is my way of being strong,

It may not be the best you've read,

Nor the worst I've heard it said,

To express myself and how I feel,

Sweet as honey, cold as steel,

This is something I do for me,

Without it, I, as me cease to be.

Has Anyone Ever Loved You?

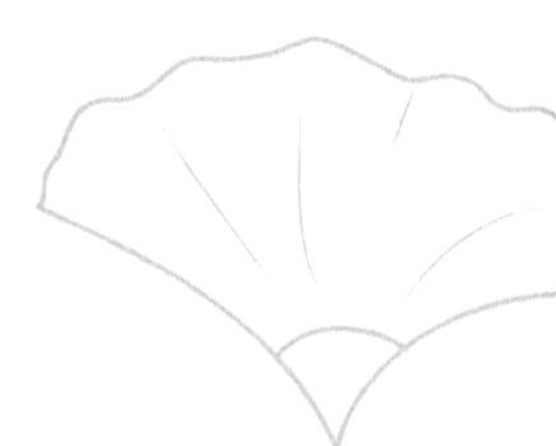

Has anyone ever loved you, knowing you to the core?

Realizing the significance of everything that's come before?

Has anyone held you valuing what they hold?

Has anyone ever listened the story be retold?

Has anyone ever loved you, drinking in the night?

Standing firm before you in the morning's light?

Has anyone ever caressed you with amazement in their eyes?

When nurtured, your potential fully realized?

Has anyone ever vowed they would be your last?

Making it a priority to disengage the past?

Has anyone ever seen your being full and aware?

Rising in the moment intimacy to share?

Has anyone ever loved you as no other had before?

Has anyone stood firm as you were shaken to the core?

Has anyone been bold enough to tame the turbulent winds?

To build a bridge in order your chasm to transcend.

Has anyone ever endeavored to be worthy of your love?

Despite insecurities, accept and rise above?

Has anyone ever known it would take little to impress,

For the woman you've become ties the bows on her own dress.

Has anyone ever realized they simply need to be,

Precisely who they are, a separate identity?

Has anyone ever loved you?

Reflection

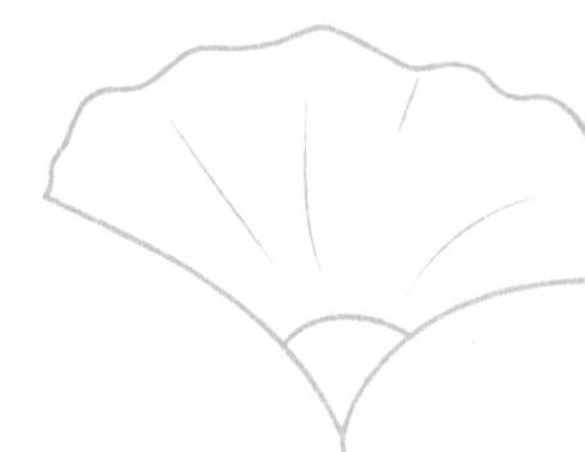

Reflecting from the mirror the woman I see,

Radiates strength, power, and beauty,

A body shaped, curvy and round,

Stretch marks a history without a sound,

Breasts resting from gravity's pull,

Tummy soft, a reminder of my womb being full,

This evidence of life brought forth,

Reminding me of a mother's worth.

Ciera

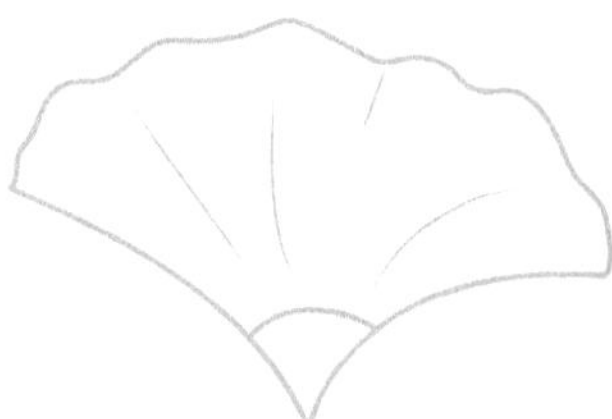

Cascades of water flowing over her head,

Eyelashes form droplets,

As she blinks, they do wed,

A messenger from a place far behind,

Watching her, discovery fills heart and mind,

Bringing me back to this world through her eyes,

Bright, new full of surprise,

Unaware of the magic she brings,

For she is simply doing little girl things.

So. Cal Blues

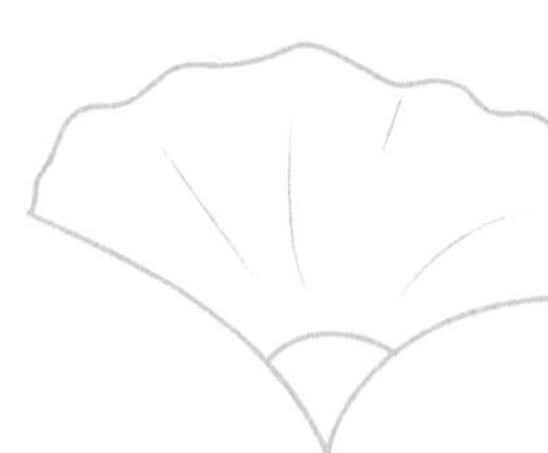

I hope someday my boys will know,

What it's like to watch falling snow,

The fun it is to snowball fight,

With the powder that fell the previous night,

Sit by the fire drinking hot cocoa

Look out the window at flurries of snow,

Parks with their toboggan runs,

The hazy lemon dot that was the sun,

To build secret tunnels in drifts oh so high,

Look at the horizon and see snow and sky,

Stomp through the drifts, skid on the ice,

Snow is a child's paradise,

There was snow the whole time that I was growing,

Winter wasn't official unless it was snowing,

I hope someday my boys will know,

What it's like to play in the snow,

To explore and experience that powdery fluff,

That makes life for grownups so very rough.

I watch as they

Smoke some drink some, snort some coke,

Talk of the past and tell some jokes,

Maybe we'll get it, maybe we won't,

But please no replays if we don't,

We'll sit at the table, go for a walk,

We may even go around the block,

Let's not waste our time it's too precious to spare,

We'll take the car, who will dare?

Forget the car, there's a store real close,

On reality can you overdose?

It's okay though we aren't in a car,

I know there's a store here not very far,

We'll walk together laughing and singing,

We'll dance in the streets our hips just a swinging,

The fresh air will do us some good,

We'll remember times when things were as they should,

No pavement, no sewers, no gangs, and no smog,

When kids swam in ponds and chased after frogs,

Will things ever turn to the way they should be?

Could things get worse, could they possibly?

As time goes on what will we do?

Stay where we are, simply mildew?

Or will we fight staff in hand?

Is it worth it to see earth- fresh land?

Will we turn our backs, and walk away?

I'm not sure I want to stay.

I don't care to be around and watch,

As the world creates its biggest blotch,

Shall I ignore and turn away,

Pull the curtain and hide during the day?

Sit up wondering late at night,

Gray is everywhere, what happened to black and white?

It all seems so intense to me,

Is change worth it or should we just let it be.

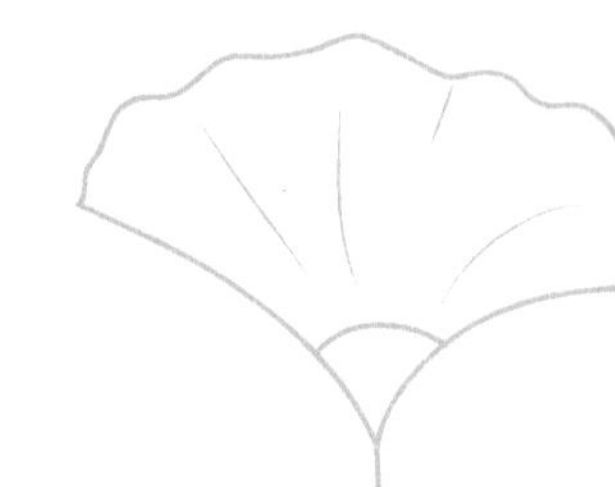

Soaring

Standing there holding onto your string,

A gentle tug and you know the next thing?

My feet left the ground you were soaring so high,

Flapping my wings, I began to fly,

Yet flapping wings a string cannot hold,

Do I dare drop the string?

Be I that bold?

With a deep breath the string fell toward the earth.

Now I could give my flight all I was worth.

As I struggled against currents, afraid to look down,

For I was far above the ground,

Glancing up, you beckoned to me,

Joining you, the view is spectacular to see.

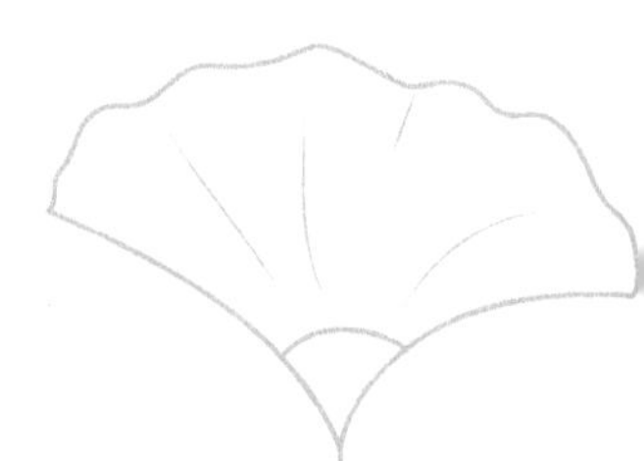

I Wait

As I lay in the dark,

I feel it come,

Anxiety, loneliness,

Longing for a loving caress,

Warm breath on the back of my neck,

An arm folding around to draw me close,

The curve of my body aligned,

My anxiety resigned,

Not just any,

Yours,

Your calmness, peaceful annoyance, balance,

Your easy temperate flow,

My soil softens,

To give place where feelings grow,

Watering me with your spirit,

Calming, soothing, yet stimulating annoyance,

Not with desire, simply acceptance,

Missing what I have not had,

Accepting your soothing spirit as enough,

Fullness never completely aligning as lovers,

Even fuller if we do,

To have you know me,

To feel your breath on my face,

My neck,

To have your energy, soothing my enthusiasm,

My enthusiasm stimulating your spirit,

Causing balance,

Knowing you, in the dark with me,

Not to rescue me,

To sooth me, calming my anxiety,

Breathing on my neck,

My face.

I wait.

Chicken Pox

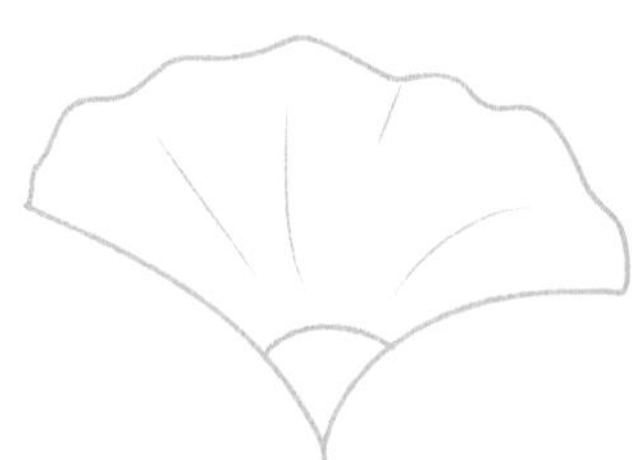

In the winter of eighty-three,

Someone is testing my sanity,

They began on his back,

Then his chest,

This morning they covered all the rest,

Those pimply red little spots,

Commonly known as chicken pox,

I had hoped Noah would coincide,

This it seems I've been denied,

No spots on Noah have I seen,

Chances are awfully lean,

That spots on Noah will not appear,

What will happen is very clear,

As spots on Jerry dry up and go,

Noah's spots will begin to show,

For what will seem an eternity,

Spots before my eyes I'll see,

Calamine lotion is out to stay,

Until these spots go away.

The Desert at Night

This house is so quiet and so still…

Something the city could never fulfill,

Nights in the city just don't seem right,

But I've always loved the desert at night,

Silhouettes of Joshua Trees,

The rustling of the tumbleweeds,

The brisk wind that chaps my face,

Even has its own place,

It shows the Creator is in command,

For it is His way of cleansing the land,

Boldly blowing afternoon and eve,

As darkness comes, it silently leaves,

In the darkness lights catch my eye,

I lift my face to the sky,

Making me thankful I can see,

The miracles of God's mastery.

Her

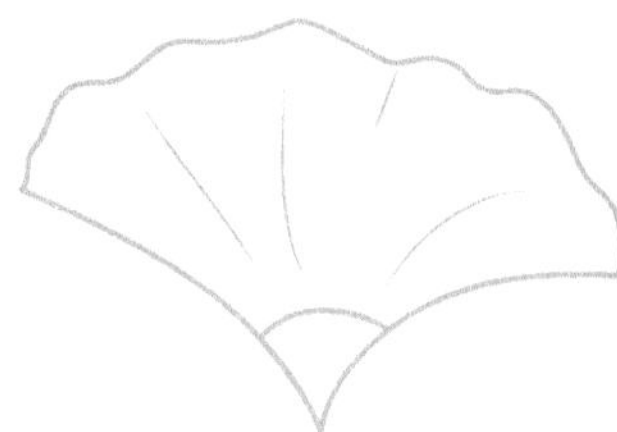

Looking at her do you see?

The woman she has grown to be?

Feelings for so long denied,

Refuse in the shadows to reside,

Not aloof,

Nor cold as stone,

Desires rise,

Hers to own,

Feelings, urges deep inside of her,

Give so much pleasure when they stir,

Erogenous fulfillment with this man,

Freeing the passion,

As nothing else can,

Expressions of intimacy,

Her womanly essence,

Unbridled and free.

Her Twenty Years Previous

Looking at her do you see,

The woman she has grown to be?

Feelings she tried to hide,

No longer can be denied,

She is not as cold as stone,

She has desires of her own,

The emotions deep inside of her,

Give so much pleasure when they stir,

She welcomes the love of her man,

He frees her as nothing else can,

The love passionately mild,

Transforming a woman from a child.

Free to Be

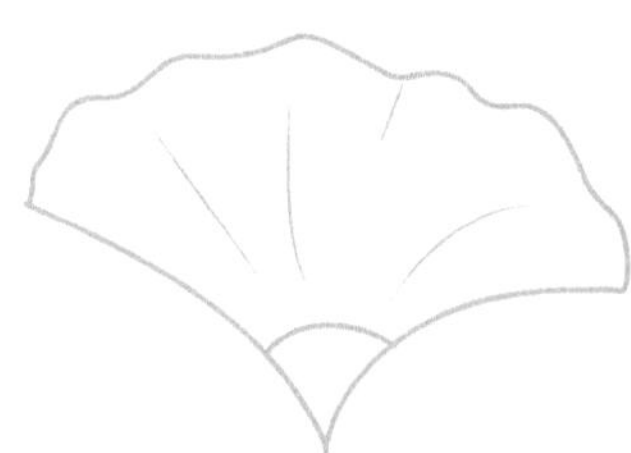

Keep holding me with an open hand,

Without constraint

Free to land,

Share with me solace and rest,

Gathering twigs,

With you I will nest,

A harmonious sanctuary for we two,

No other will taste what I have for you,

With room free to grow,

The full essence of my being you alone will know.

Release me, little one, who wants to make things right,

Desiring to stand up straight and tall,

No longer to take flight,

The point is proven here, within the lion's den,

Having stood tall, unwavering, the child now may mend,

Be gone; allow the grownup remaining to truly be,

To find attraction in someone willing to love acceptingly,

Point now proven, walk away so very proud and tall,

Resting, safe, little one, behind my fortressed wall,

Beasts shall no longer roam within this peaceful hearth,

As I fully comprehend the value of my worth.